TO COME WHEN CALLED

R
RINGPRESS

Published by **Ringpress Books**,
a division of Interpet Publishing,
Vincent Lane, Dorking, Surrey, RH4 3YX, UK
Tel: 01306 873822   Fax: 01306 876712
email: sales@interpet.co.uk

ISBN 1 86054 296 4

First published 2002 All rights reserved.

CARTOONS: Russell Jones
DESIGN: Rob Benson

Printed and bound in Hong Kong through Printworks International Limited

CONTENTS

A POSITIVE RESPONSE

The world of dog owners is united on one subject – the need for a dog to come when he is called. Everyone wants a happy dog who responds enthusiastically to the "Come" command; nobody wants a dog who pleases himself and turns a 'deaf' ear when he is called. It does not matter whether you own a huge Irish Wolfhound or a tiny Yorkshire Terrier, life is a misery if your dog cannot be trusted to return to your side.

ESTABLISHING CONTROL

Despite thousands of years of domestication, the dog still sees himself as a pack animal. In the wild, the pack always has a leader who makes the decisions and enjoys top-ranking privileges. In a domestic situation, it is essential that your dog sees you, his human owner, as his leader. This means that the dog is willing to comply with your wishes.

In order to make the relationship work in relative harmony, you do not want a situation where you must compel the dog to obey. The aim is to have a dog who *wants* to be with you, and is motivated to do as you ask. In most cases where relations break down, the dog simply prefers to follow his own agenda, or the owner has, unknowingly, taught the dog to stay away (see page 22).

THE RELIABLE COMPANION

Make sure you build up a good relationship with your dog right from the beginning so he is eager to please.

Be consistent in your training. If, for example, you tell your dog off for going on the sofa one day, and then let him get away with it the next time, you will end up with a confused dog who will start to question your leadership.

During adolescence, most dogs, especially males, will challenge your leadership. You may find that your dog suddenly starts to disobey you, and is very keen on pleasing himself. This is the time to go back to basics, and work on all your training exercises. Be firm, fair and consistent, and your dog will grow out of his 'teenage' phase and become a reliable companion that you can take anywhere – and will return to you on command.

THE RIGHT START

If you have a new puppy, you can start your recall training from the moment you get your pup home. If you are taking on an older dog, or simply brushing up on training, the following points are equally relevant.

THE NAME GAME

Everyone has their own ideas about naming pets, and, doubtless, many hours will be spent debating the choice. However, if you want your dog to respond to his name, do not make things too complicated. "Aloysius, come" is a terrible mouthful, and is unlikely to prompt a quick response; "Shep, come" is short and distinct, and a dog will find it much easier to learn.

QUENTIN ALEXANDER HERCULES SMITH

It is also important to be consistent in the way you address your dog. "Sam", "Sammy" or "Samuel" may mean the same to you, but it could be bewildering to a dog who is responding purely to the sound of a word.

REAPING REWARDS

In all training, the trick is for your dog to *want* to do what you ask. Before you start formal training, find out what treat your dog most enjoys. With many, a food treat will be the greatest incentive, but some prefer a game with a toy. Decide what makes your dog tick, and every time he responds correctly, give a treat in the form of food or a game. As training progresses, the rewards can be given on a more random basis.

TONE OF VOICE

Your voice is a great training aid. Make yourself sound really exciting and your dog will want to come to you. Give lots of praise, and your dog will know he has done well.

BODY LANGUAGE

Dogs are much more attuned to body language than humans. A dog will be able to sense your mood by the way you move, and this can be used to your advantage when you are training. If you want your dog to come, crouch down to his level, open out your arms, and welcome him. Give him a pat or a stroke to reward him.

TRAINING ENVIRONMENT

A dog is easily distracted by things going on around him. An interesting scent, an unexpected noise, or another dog appearing on the horizon are all temptations that are hard to resist.

TO COME WHEN CALLED

TEACH YOUR DOG

A dog should see the recall as a fun part of training.

When you start training, try to find an environment that is as free from distractions as possible. Give your dog every chance to concentrate and respond correctly before introducing additional challenges.

BAD VIBES

The aim is to have a dog that *wants* to come to you, so you must ensure your dog does not associate a negative experience with the "Come" command or he will see no point in responding.

Do not call your dog to you and then immediately give him a bath or some form of medication. If you do this, you can be sure that your dog will learn to stay away from you rather than risking something unpleasant. Equally, when you start taking your dog out for walks off-lead, do not call him to you, and immediately put him on the lead. All you have taught your dog is that "Come" means the end of the walk, and he will quickly learn that he can prolong the walk by staying away from you.

Remember, "Come" *always* means fun.

FIRST STEPS

Puppies have an inbuilt instinct to follow, so make use of this from the beginning.

FOLLOW MY LEADER

At four to five weeks of age, as puppies become more independent from their mother, they will generally become more focused on the person that cares for them. Most litters will latch on to their breeder, and a call of "Puppies, come" will elicit a response, particularly if a bowl of food is being offered. The puppies get accustomed to seeing human feet and legs, and will be happy to follow their new human leader.

When your puppy arrives in his new home, he will be eager to find some security. Generally, this will mean that the puppy will attempt to follow you wherever you go – and tripping over the puppy becomes a regular pastime.

There are distinct benefits to be gained from this behaviour. At every opportunity, use your puppy's name – then, as he follows you, give the command "Come". In no

Use your puppy's name and the command "Come" at every opportunity.

time, the puppy will have learnt to respond to his name, and he will associate the command "Come" with following you.

While your puppy is keen to follow you, go into the garden and practise the "Come" command. This will build up your puppy's acceptance of the command in a more challenging environment.

FOLLOW THAT FOOD BOWL!

Mealtimes are the high spot of a dog's day, and they can also be used for training both puppies and older dogs. For this exercise you need to enlist the help of another member of the family or a friend.

- Prepare the meal, and then ask someone to hold on to the dog at the far end of a room.
- Give the command "Come", and allow the dog to be released.
- Praise the dog as he comes to you.
- The dog can now have his meal – he has earnt it!

WHISTLE STOP

Association plays a strong part in the learning process, and it can be used to reinforce the "Come" command. Buy a whistle, available from most pet stores, and command your dog to "Sit" as you offer his food bowl. Then give a couple of short blasts on the whistle. The dog will quickly learn to associate the sound of the whistle with food. Make sure you are consistent, and always give the same number of blasts on the whistle each time you use it.

When you start doing recall training, use the whistle, and as your dog comes to you, reward him with a food treat. This keeps the whistle-food connection in his mind, and he will be eager to come to you every time he hears the whistle.

Do not neglect your verbal commands to back up the whistle. The aim is to have a dog that will respond to all types of commands in all situations.

FUN RECALLS

Training should be fun for both you and your dog. You can enlist a helper to play a recall game.

- The helper holds on to the dog, and you place yourself a short distance away.
- Call your dog, and the helper immediately releases the dog so he can respond to the "Come" command. As soon as the dog reaches you, give him lots of praise.
- The game is then reversed, with the dog being called back the other way.

Most dogs love this game. If you are training a puppy, be careful that he does not get too over-excited, and also remember that a young puppy has a short concentration span and he will get tired very easily.

11

GAINING CONTROL

O nce you have an enthusiastic response to the "Come" command, the next stage is to introduce a more formal structure to the exercise. Training should be conducted in a distraction-free environment, such as the garden, but if you are training a puppy, do not neglect the importance of going further afield for socialisation once he has completed his vaccination course.

SIT

This is one of the first lessons to teach. Start by holding a treat above your dog's nose, and, as he looks up, he will generally go into the Sit position. Sometimes this takes a little patience, but as soon as your dog responds correctly, use the command "Sit" and reward him. Practise in a variety of situations, and when your dog clearly understands the command, give the treats on a random basis.

When your dog is used to his collar and lead, practise the "Sit" command with the dog on-lead.

Practise the Sit command in a variety of different situations.

WAIT

This exercise should be built up in stages. Do not be tempted to rush or you will end up with a dog that keeps getting up to follow you.

- Start off with your dog on-lead in the Sit. Give the command "Wait" and take one step to the side. You can also use a hand signal – a flat palm held towards the dog – to back up the verbal command.

As your dog gains confidence, go to the end of the lead, and give the command "Wait".

- Step back to your dog's side, and praise him quietly while he stays in the Sit.
- Stand in front of your dog, give the command "Wait" and take one step back. Use your hand signal, command "Wait" again, and stay where you are for approximately 30 seconds before returning to your dog. Praise your dog before allowing him to break position. Then give a release command, such as "OK", and reward him with a game or a treat.
- Repeat the exercise, stepping behind your dog, to the right of your puppy, and then walking in a circle around him while he remains in the Sit.
- When you are confident that your dog is staying in position, go in front of your dog, command "Wait", and take a few steps back to the end of the lead. Turn around so you are facing away from your dog. Repeat the command "Wait", and stay in position for approximately 30 seconds before returning.
- Build up the time your dog will "Wait" in easy stages.

TRAINING TIP

In most cases, handlers are encouraged to be full of enthusiastic praise when the dog has responded correctly. But this can be counter-productive when teaching Wait and Stay exercises. The dog starts to anticipate the praise, and breaks position to come and greet you.

- When you return to your dog, keep your body as still as possible and stand at your dog's side.
- Say "good dog" very quietly and calmly, praising him while he remains in the Sit.
- When the exercise is finished, give a release command, such as "OK" or "Finish", so that the dog understands he is free to break position.
- Now you can have a game with your dog, rewarding him for completing the exercise.

TRAINING LINE

This is a very simple piece of equipment, but it is an invaluable aid when teaching the recall. Buy a length of cord, approximately 9 ft in length. Coil it up, and then attach one end of the cord to your dog's collar.

Repeat your "Wait" exercises, first going to half the length of the line, and then going to the full extent. The training line means that you can leave your dog at a greater distance, but you still maintain control. If you have worked on the "Wait" in easy stages, your dog should accept this progression quite happily.

Always exercise great care when using a training line. A dog can easily get tangled up, particularly if you are training a boisterous puppy. If this is the case, it is advisable to keep working with the dog on-lead until you are confident that you have full control.

Once your dog is responding to the "Sit" and "Wait", it is tempting to move on to a full recall, calling your dog to you from the Sit.

However, one of the major problems in the recall exercise is the dog anticipating the "Come" command, so it is better to keep "Sit" and "Wait" as separate exercises until your dog is completely steady in the Wait.

TO COME WHEN CALLED

PUTTING IT TOGETHER

If you have followed the stage-by-stage training programme, you should now have a dog that responds to the recall in fun situations, and is steady in the Sit and Wait. Now is the time to put the elements of the exercise together. It is a good idea to start off with your dog on the training line, and only try him off-lead when he has mastered the complete exercise.

THE RECALL EXERCISE

- Start with your dog in the Sit. Command "Wait", backing it up with a hand signal, and leave your dog.
- Walk off in a positive manner. If you creep away, expecting your dog to follow, he almost certainly will.
- When you get to the end of the training line, turn and face your dog. Command "Wait" again.
- Call your dog – "Shep, come" – and give lots of praise when your dog comes to you.
- As your dog becomes confident, you can introduce a "Sit" as he comes to you. But to begin with, work on a strong, positive response to "Come" before attempting this.

RECALL OFF-LEAD

This should follow exactly the same pattern as the recall using the training line. However, it is important to be even more aware of your body language and tone of voice so that your dog has a crystal-clear understanding of what is required.

- Repeat the "Wait" command as you leave your dog, using a deep, firm tone of voice.
- Walk 8-10 ft away, keeping your arms to your sides so that you do not accidentally give any encouraging signals for your dog to follow.
- Stand still, facing away from your dog, and command "Wait".
- Turn and face your dog, and command "Wait", backing it up with the hand signal.
- Open out your arms to welcome your dog in, and give the command "Come" in a bright, exciting voice. When your dog responds, give lots of praise, and reward him with a treat or a game with his toy.

Give a positive command when you command your dog to "Wait".

Open your arms and make yourself sound exciting so that your dog wants to come to you.

INTRODUCING DISTRACTIONS

When you are teaching a new exercise, it is important to work in an environment that is as free from distractions as possible. However, when you are confident that your dog understands what is required, you will need to introduce distractions so that he learns to respond to you in all situations.

FOCUSING ATTENTION

Ask a member of the family to stand to one side as you do the recall exercise. Your dog's attention will obviously be distracted, so you must work all the harder at focusing his attention on you. Make sure your dog is listening to you, and give a firm "Wait" command. When you command "Come", make yourself sound irresistible so your dog bounds up to you.

Then, ask your assistant to walk up and down while you repeat the recall exercise. If your dog shows any hesitation in coming to you, jump up and down, and sound as though you are inviting your dog to join in a game – few dogs can resist the prospect of play.

When your dog is showing good concentration, go to a quiet place and work on the recall exercise (using the training line). When you are happy with your dog's progress, attempt the exercise off-lead, making sure the place you choose is completely safe, and away from any traffic.

It is important that your dog realises that he must respond to the "Come" command in all situations – not just when it is part of a formal recall exercise. Keep practising at home, both in the house and in the garden, so that your dog learns that "Come" means that he must stop whatever he is doing and come and find you. The moment he responds, give lots of praise, and reward him with a treat or a game. The dog must understand that coming to you is *always* the best thing on offer.

TRAINING CLASSES

A training class is an excellent place for your dog to learn to work amid distractions. Make sure you check out the training club before you take your dog along. Any use of force or compulsion should be avoided at all costs. The training ethic should be motivation and reward.

To begin with, the other dogs will be a huge temptation, and your dog will struggle to concentrate. Make sure you have plenty of treats, and a toy to have a game with. This will help to focus your dog's attention on you.

As your dog becomes more used to the environment, you will be able to work on the recall with other dogs in close proximity. When your dog is working off-lead, responding to the "Come", rather than rushing off to the other dogs, you will know that you are making real progress!

CLICKER TRAINING

This is an increasingly popular method of training, where the sound of the clicker is used to shape or reinforce desirable behaviour. The dog learns to associate the sound of the clicker with a reward; it is the signal that tells him he is responding correctly and a reward will follow. Clicker-training is particularly useful in treating dogs who have already learned to ignore whistles and other calls for attention.

It is essential to get the timing absolutely right when you are using a clicker, so it is a good idea to go to a training club that specialises in clicker training.

TRAINING TIP

Find out which is your dog's favourite toy, and then keep it specifically for training sessions. This gives the toy special value, and your dog will see a game with his 'training' toy as a top reward.

PARK LIFE

The greatest test is when you allow your dog to free run in the park, and then call him back to you. If you have progressed through all the stages of training, this should not prove a major hurdle.

Arm yourself with lots of treats and take your dog's training toy. If you have been using a whistle as part of your recall (see page 11), make sure you bring it with you.

Allow your dog off-lead, and, after a few minutes, call him back. Give him a treat or have a game with his toy, and then let him go off again. Do not allow your dog to roam too far afield. Keep calling him back and rewarding him, so that he enjoys the interaction rather than seeing it as a restriction on his freedom.

HERE BOY!

COMING BOSS!

If your dog runs too far ahead, give a couple of short blasts on the whistle to attract his attention, and then call him in.

Always praise your dog when he returns to you, even if the response has not been quite as instant as you would like. Never punish your dog when he returns – no matter what he has been doing.

You may think you are reprimanding your dog for being slow to respond to you. But a dog's mind works differently. He lives in the present, and he will think that coming back to you results in a telling off. Next time, he may not bother to come back.

TO COME WHEN CALLED

TRAINING TIP

If your dog runs off when you call him, never chase after him. As far as your dog is concerned, this is a great game, and he will prolong it indefinitely. However, a dog is strongly motivated by seeing his owner run off in the opposite direction, and so if your dog tries to run off, turn the tables on him – and he will come running after you.

Remember, always reward your dog when he comes to you, even if you have had to work hard for it!

Always reward your dog for coming –
even if you don't think he deserves it!

PROBLEM SOLVING

Training is an on-going business, and your dog will benefit from – and enjoy – continuing interaction with his owner. Problems arise for many reasons, but the most common are:

- The dog has never fully understood what is required.
- The dog is not sufficiently motivated to respond.
- The owner has, unknowingly, 'taught' the incorrect response.

In the following case studies, we look at problems that have arisen in training and methods of tackling them.

THE SCENT HOUND

Judy, a two-year-old Beagle, is in her element when she is out on a walk. Tail up and nose to the ground, Judy is 'deaf' to all calls when she is on a scent.

FINDING A SOLUTION

Dogs have a tremendously powerful sense of smell, and investigating all the different scents on a walk is a huge source of enjoyment.

The secret of curing Judy's 'deafness' to the recall was to find a way of interrupting her train of thought so that she remembered she had an owner she wanted to respond to.

STAGE 1: Judy's owner was advised to go back to basics and to work on the whistle recall. The whistle was used at mealtimes to build up a strong association.

- After a little trial and error, cheese was found to be Judy's favourite food, and so cheese treats were reserved exclusively for practising the recall exercise.
- Judy was put in one part of the house, and her owner whistled for her. As soon as Judy found her owner, she was given a treat. This turned the recall into a fun game, and Judy was not distracted by a scent.

STAGE 2: The next step was to repeat the exercise in the garden, where there was a limited chance of Judy being distracted by a scent.

- When Judy was responding well, she was tried in the park on a training line. Judy was allowed to go to the length of the line, and when she had clearly found a scent, the whistle was used – with treats at the ready.
- When Judy started to respond more positively to the whistle, she was tried off-lead, and the prospect of a cheese treat was enough to bring her back to her owner's side.

SUMMARY

A dog with a very keen nose is always going to be tempted to stray, and Judy's progress was steady to begin with. However, she learnt that two blasts of the whistle meant her favourite food treat was on hand, and eventually she could be trusted off-lead.

PROBLEM SOLVING

THE GARDEN SAGA

Whenever Chester, a nine-month-old Golden Retriever, was let out into the garden, he refused to come back in again. To begin with, it seemed a bit of a game, but the behaviour quickly became an established habit.

FINDING A SOLUTION

There were two aspects to this behaviour. Chester had clearly lost respect for his owner, and, at nine months, he had decided to test the boundaries and see how far he could go. Secondly, Chester had made up his mind that going into the house represented the end of his freedom, and he was not prepared to give that up without a fight.

STAGE I: Chester's owner was asked to allocate ten minutes a day to running through all the basic training exercises. This was done in the garden, and included a few fun recalls from one end of the garden to the other. The session always ended with a good game of tug with Chester's favourite rope toy. This helped to re-establish good relations between dog and owner.

STAGE 2: Chester had to learn that coming into the house was not the last thing he wanted to do.

- The training session ended with a game, and as they were playing, Chester's owner edged her way into the house. Chester was so busy playing tug, he forgot his usual resistance.
- In the house, Chester's owner continued the game for a few minutes, and then swapped the toy for a food treat.

STAGE 3: Chester's owner laid a trail of treats in the garden that led through the door and into the house.

- Using the command "Find", Chester had great fun following the trail into the house where he was given lots of praise and a game with his toy.
- Next, the trail of treats went into the house and ended with Chester finding his favourite toy.

STAGE 4: Chester's owner started doing some recalls in the garden, gradually moving closer towards the door. When Chester responded correctly, he was rewarded with a game.

- Getting Chester to come back into the house when he was called was relatively easy. Chester's owner stood on the doorstep, with the toy, and called him in. As soon as Chester responded, they went into the house and had a play session.

SUMMARY

Chester needed to respect his owner, and this went a long way to stopping his challenging behaviour. He also had to learn that coming when called was a rewarding experience. When both these lessons were fully absorbed, it put a stop to Chester's undesirable behaviour.

DOG DISTRACTIONS

Bobby, a four-year-old Jack Russell, was rehomed from a rescue shelter. Although he was generally well behaved, all his training was forgotten whenever he met another dog. Despite his owner's repeated calls, Bobby only had eyes for his latest canine friend.

FINDING A SOLUTION

Bobby had got into the habit of pleasing himself every time he met up with another dog, and so the most important aspect of retraining was to break this pattern of behaviour.

STAGE I: If a dog is outside your control, you have no hope of correcting him. So, to begin with, Bobby was not allowed off the lead when he was in the park.

• Bobby was allowed to meet other dogs, but his owner decided when to end the 'conversation'. A command of "Leave" was used, and when Bobby paid attention to his owner, he was given a treat.

STAGE 2: Bobby's owner enrolled at the local dog training club. This gave Bobby the opportunity to meet other dogs in a controlled environment.
- He worked on-lead, but as his concentration improved, he started doing recalls off-lead. Bobby was rewarded with a treat and a game with a toy.

STAGE 3: Bobby's owner concentrated on recalls in the garden. Initially a treat was used, but as Bobby became more focused on the toy, his reward was a game. Bobby would be more likely to respond to a toy when he was in the park, and would, hopefully, go from his game with another dog to a game with his owner.

STAGE 4: Bobby's owner recruited a friend who had a well-behaved dog that was reliable on the recall.
- The dogs were allowed to play together, and then the owners called them back.
- The more experienced dog responded correctly, and so Bobby had no one left to play with.
- His owner's command, coupled with the incentive of a game, worked and Bobby responded to the recall.
- When the two dogs were playing together, Bobby was called first, and, from choice, he left the dog to come and play with his owner. This was the turning point, and Bobby can now be trusted to return to his owner.

SUMMARY
When Bobby was kept on-lead, he lost the opportunity to run off. He was given controlled exposure to other dogs, and his attention was refocused on his owner. In time, these elements worked together, and Bobby responded to the recall because he *wanted* to be with his owner.

TEACH YOUR DOG

THE END OF THE ROAD

Dell, a five-year-old Weimaraner bitch, loved her walks –
so much so that she refused to come to her owner when it
was time to go home. They tended to go on the same
walks most days, so Dell knew precisely when to stray
further afield.

FINDING A SOLUTION

Dell was no fool. If she didn't respond to the recall at the
end of a walk, the outing went on for longer. The short-
term plan was to confuse Dell so she didn't know when to
start playing up. In the long term, she needed an incentive
to return to her owner on command.

STAGE 1: Dell's owner was advised to work on his dog's strengths rather than getting frustrated by her disobedience.

- Dell loved retrieve games, and so Dell's owner selected a favourite tug toy to use for a game after a recall.
- Training was confined to the garden, and when Dell responded correctly, she had a game of tug followed by a couple of retrieves. This made for a great play session, but it also gave Dell an incentive to keep returning to her owner.

STAGE 2: Dell's owner found different walks. In fact, he enjoyed the change of scene, and Dell, feeling slightly less secure in new surroundings, was more focused on her owner.

- Throughout the walk, Dell was called back to her owner, and was rewarded with a game and a couple of retrieves.
- Obviously, in a new environment, Dell had no landmarks to tell her when the walk was coming to an end. So, on some occasions when she was called in, she was put on the lead for a few minutes and then let off again.
- On other occasions, she was called in, had a game and was allowed to run free again.
- The outing was concluded without the habitual battle of wills, which was a major breakthrough.

SUMMARY

Dogs appreciate variety and a bright dog will soon make capital out of a dull routine. Dell's owner also realised that he could not walk along, taking no notice of his dog and then expect her to come back when commanded. Dell enjoyed the new interaction with her owner, and she associated coming back to him with having fun, rather than seeing it as the signal that her outing was at an end.

TO COME WHEN CALLED

FINAL NOTE

There is no mystery to recall training. If you work hard at it, and reward your dog, he should be happy to respond.

Remember the three golden rules:

- Be the boss
- Be consistent
- Make it fun.

A well-behaved dog who always comes when he is called is a pleasure to own. A good recall is also the key to going on to compete in other canine sports, such as Agility and Flyball. Who knows – you may even be tempted to have a go at Competitive Obedience...

Happy recalling!